Searchlight
BOOKS™

Getting into Government

Exploring the

Judicial Branch

by Danielle Smith-Llera

Lerner Publications ✦ Minneapolis

Text copyright © 2020 by Lerner Publishing Group, Inc.

Lerner Publications
An imprint of Lerner Publishing Group, Inc.
241 First Avenue North
Minneapolis, MN 55401 USA

For reading levels and more information, look up this title
at www.lernerbooks.com.

Main body text set in Adrianna Regular 14/20.
Typeface provided by Chank.

Library of Congress Cataloging-in-Publication Data

Names: Smith-Llera, Danielle, 1971– author.
Title: Exploring the judicial branch / by Danielle Smith-Llera.
Description: Minneapolis : Lerner Publications, [2019] | Series: Searchlight Books™—
    Getting into Government | Includes bibliographical references
and index.
Identifiers: LCCN 2018059341 (print) | LCCN 2018060267
    (ebook) | ISBN 9781541556782 (eb pdf) | ISBN 9781541555884 (lb : alk. paper) |
    ISBN 9781541574793 (pb : alk. paper)
Subjects: LCSH: Courts—United States—Juvenile literature. | Justice, Administration of—
    United States—Juvenile literature. | Judicial power—United States—Juvenile literature.
Classification: LCC KF8700 (ebook) | LCC KF8700 .S589 2019 (print) | DDC 347.73—
    dc23

LC record available at https://lccn.loc.gov/2018059341

Manufactured in the United States of America
1-46043-43366-4/4/2019

Contents

Chapter 1

INSIDE THE JUDICIAL BRANCH

In 1984, Gregory Lee Johnson set the American flag on fire. He was protesting government leaders. He was arrested because it was against the law to damage the American flag. But Johnson didn't agree with that law. He believed he should be free to protest as he did. The judicial branch takes over when people disagree about laws. Johnson went to court and defended his actions.

Gregory Lee Johnson's flag burning became national news.

Inside the Courtroom

Judges are the most powerful members of the judicial branch. They are in charge of the court and decide if a person broke the law. During a trial like Johnson's, the judge listens carefully to the facts of a case. Sometimes a group of people, called a jury, listens too. The judge and

jury decide who is right. Then the judge decides what will happen if the person broke a law. A judge in Texas decided that Johnson broke the law and would have to pay a fine and go to prison. But that wasn't the end of the case.

Judges work in courtrooms.

A Pyramid

The courts in the judicial branch are set up in different levels like a pyramid. If people disagree with a judge's decision, they can ask for another judge in a higher court to hear the case again. Johnson took his case to a higher court. This higher court disagreed with the lower court's decision and changed the ruling.

The lowest level of federal courts are district courts.

The Supreme Court's ruling is the final decision on a case.

The Supreme Court is the country's highest court. Nine judges, called justices, listen to cases from across the nation. They often choose cases where lower courts disagreed. They heard Johnson's flag-burning case after two Texas courts disagreed.

At least half the justices must agree for the Supreme Court to reach a decision. Five of the justices decided that Johnson had a right to protest by burning the flag. He won the case.

That's a Fact!

The Supreme Court makes decisions for everyone in the United States. But for a long time, its justices did not look like a lot of the people in the country. Only white men served on the Supreme Court for almost two hundred years. Thurgood Marshall became the first African American justice in 1967. In 1981, Sandra Day O'Connor became the first female justice. The court has started to represent all the people it serves.

Justice Sonia Sotomayor has been on the Supreme Court since 2009. She is the first Latina justice on the Supreme Court.

Chapter 2

JUDICIAL BRANCH POWERS

The legislative branch is made up of the United States Congress.

The judicial branch is one of three branches, or parts, of the government. The others are the legislative and the executive branches. The legislative branch passes laws. The executive branch includes the president and the people who work for the president. This branch enforces laws. But the judicial branch has the power to decide what the laws mean.

The Court Systems

The United States has federal courts and state courts. Most trials take place in state courts. Each state has its own set of lower and higher courts. They deal with people breaking state laws such as driving above the speed limit. If a person hurts another person in the same state, the trial usually takes place in a state court.

Cases where one person stole from another person in the state would go to state court.

ONE FEDERAL LAW SAYS THAT EVERYBODY MUST BE TREATED FAIRLY NO MATTER HOW OLD A PERSON IS.

Federal courts hear cases that deal with people in more than one state. Federal courts have another important job. They hear cases where federal laws, or laws for everyone in the nation, may have been broken. Federal courts can make decisions that affect everyone in the country.

Protecting Freedoms

Federal judges use the rights listed in the United States Constitution to guide their decisions. These rights appear in amendments to the Constitution. Amendments are changes to the Constitution. Federal courts hear cases where people believe that others have taken away their rights.

The US Constitution was written in 1787.

Making decisions is difficult for federal judges. They listen during trials to understand exactly what happened in each case. They review what other judges have decided in similar cases. They also have to think about what the Constitution's words mean. For example, the Constitution protects the freedom of people to express their opinions. Does that freedom include burning a flag? Judges have to decide.

A judge's decisions may upset some people. People who disagree with a decision might share their opinions by protesting.

Government Affects You

Social media lets people connect with one another. But sometimes it is used to send hurtful messages. Passing laws against this kind of behavior is hard because the Constitution protects the freedom of speech. However, these messages can be harmful. The Supreme Court decided that students cannot express opinions that take away the rights of other students. Laws give schools the power to make sure social media activity doesn't make another student feel unsafe at school.

What can you do to make sure you and your friends are staying safe and fair online?

Thurgood Marshall was an important figure in the fight for equality in schools. Later, he became the Supreme Court's first African American justice.

Keeping Laws Fair

Courts do more than decide who is right in a case. Trials allow judges to see if laws are fair. Judges can ask for laws to be changed or removed if they decide a law takes away a person's constitutional rights.

For example, some old laws allowed states to separate students into different schools based on race. The Supreme Court decided that the government must treat all people equally. The court's decision meant that separating students took away peoples' rights under the Constitution.

Chapter 3

JUSTICE FOR ALL

A judge's decisions can affect peoples' lives for years. So the right men and women should get the job. Different court systems have different ways to decide who will be judges. Some states vote on judges. In other states, leaders of the state government might pick the judges. State judges serve for a set amount of time, or term. Most judges serve terms between six and ten years long.

California governor Arnold Schwarzenegger (*left*) selected Judge Carol Corrigan (*right*) to be a judge in 2005.

Sharing Power

Federal judges are chosen differently than members of
the state courts. The Constitution gives the legislative
branch the power to decide the size and shape of
the federal court system. The executive branch also
plays a role in the federal court system. This is part
of checks and balances, a system of separating
governmental powers.

The executive
branch has some
power over the
judicial branch.

Justice Brett Kavanaugh (*left*) was President Donald Trump's choice as a Supreme Court justice.

The executive and legislative branches help choose federal judges and Supreme Court justices. The president announces a choice. Then a small group of members of Congress votes to approve or reject the president's choice. After that, a larger group in Congress votes on the person. The president officially signs off on the new judge if Congress approves.

A Long Service

Federal judges can serve for the rest of their lives. Their decisions shape laws for much longer than the time that a president serves. Federal judges also keep their jobs for longer than most members of the legislative branch are in office.

Federal judges can be fired only if they break laws or do not do their jobs fairly, but this happens rarely.

The longest-serving justice was William O. Douglas, who sat on the Supreme Court for more than thirty-six years.

That's a Fact!

The president selects federal judges. But in 2000, federal judges helped decide who would be president. George W. Bush and Al Gore were running for president. The close election came down to the votes in Florida. But that state had trouble with some of its voting machines. Did the law allow for votes from those machines to be counted again in a different way? The Supreme Court decided it did not. All votes needed to be treated the same.

Bush (*left*) became the forty-third US president.

A person on trial has the right to choose whether to speak in court.

Fair Treatment for All

The Constitution gives everyone rights. People accused of breaking a law have rights. These rights protect people at the time of an arrest and continue when they stand before a judge. For example, every person has the right to a speedy trial.

Chapter 4

GET INVOLVED

You may never be inside a courtroom. But what happens in courts across the country affects every part of your life. The court's decisions help keep you safe. They protect your rights and freedoms.

Courts help protect your health. Judges have decided that drinking water must be clean. They have decided that labels on your food must list all ingredients. Judges have also decided your school must be a safe place for you to learn.

The judicial branch is protecting your rights every day at school.

You have a right to your
ideas. Someone cannot steal
another person's idea and use
it to make money.

Courts protect what people own. It is your right to
have what you own, and it is against the law for someone
else to take what is yours. Judges have decided that no
one can enter your home without permission. Judges
even protect your ideas. Schools have rules against
students who copy others' work. Adults who do the same
thing can end up in a courtroom.

Government Affects You

Your school library has many different kinds of books. The Supreme Court decided that people cannot remove books because they disagree with the content. Every September, some public libraries host Banned Books Week. They display popular books that were once removed from libraries. They celebrate that the freedom to read different kinds of information is protected by judicial branch rulings based on the Constitution.

This library celebrates books that people in the past had banned from libraries.

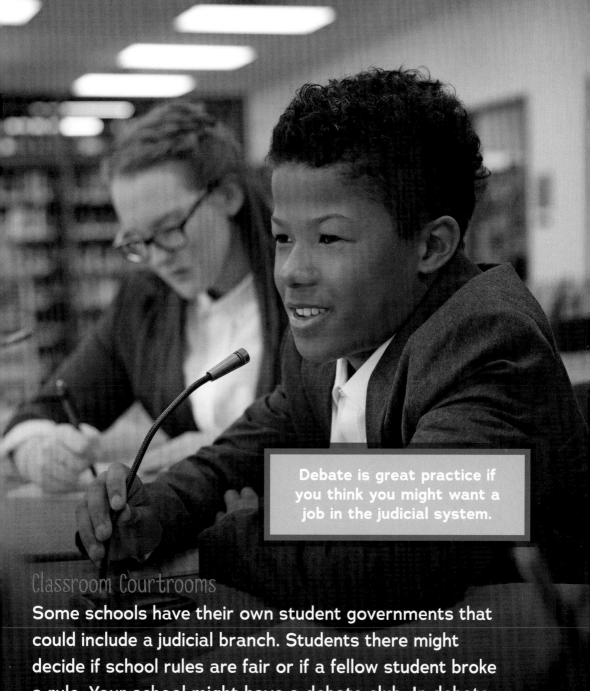

Debate is great practice if you think you might want a job in the judicial system.

Classroom Courtrooms

Some schools have their own student governments that could include a judicial branch. Students there might decide if school rules are fair or if a fellow student broke a rule. Your school might have a debate club. In debate, you can practice giving your case just as you might in a

Adults eighteen years of age or older can vote.

In some states, adults can vote for state judges. In others, they cannot. The people never vote on federal judges. But people can vote for the president and members of Congress, who will help choose federal judges. It's important to be active in government, including voting. You can learn about the people running for office even before you can vote. And you can encourage adults you know to vote.

Know your Rights

You can always learn more about the judicial system even if you aren't able to vote or take part in a student judicial system. Know the rights you have in the US Constitution. Learn more about what the courts decided on different issues. These decisions could affect you.

You can find more information about your rights and court decisions in books, on the internet, and from your parents and teachers.

Looking Ahead

For over two hundred years, judges in the judicial branch have decided how the Constitution protects the rights of all Americans. The document also says that rights listed in the Constitution are not the only ones people have. The judicial system's work will never end!

Maybe one day, you could be a part of the judicial system.

Who's Right?

Supreme Court justices can stay in the court for life. Some people think Supreme Court justices should serve for limited terms. Some do not.

Some argue that lifetime service allows justices to make the best decisions. They do not need to worry about voters' opinions to focus on the Constitution's rules.

On the other hand, justices with term limits might better reflect the opinions of the American people of the time.

Who is right? Should there be a term limit for justices? Why or why not?

Glossary

amendment: a change in the wording or meaning of the Constitution or another legal document

case: a set of facts or evidence to support one side of an argument

court: a building or room where legal cases are heard

executive: the branch of government that carries out laws and includes the president, vice president, and a presidential cabinet of advisers

federal: the national system

jury: local people who listen to a court case and decide who's innocent and who's guilty

legislative: the branch of government that makes laws and includes Congress

right: a privilege that cannot be taken away

ruling: a decision made by a court

term: a set amount of time for an elected official to hold office

Learn More about the Judicial Branch

Books

Alexander, Vincent. *Judicial Branch.* Minneapolis: Jump! 2018. Learn more about how the judicial branch works to make sure laws treat all people equally.

Krasner, Barbara. *Exploring Checks and Balances.* Minneapolis: Lerner Publications, 2020. Find out more about how the judicial branch works with the other branches of the US government.

MacCarald, Clara. *Establishing the Judicial Branch.* Lake Elmo, MN: Focus Readers, 2018. Take an in-depth look at the formation of the judicial branch during the creation of the United States.

Websites

Duckster: The Supreme Court
https://www.ducksters.com/history/us_judicial_branch.php
Explore more about the pyramid of courts in the judicial branch of the government.

Fact Monster: All about Court
https://www.factmonster.com/us/laws-and-rights/all-about-court
Step inside a courtroom to meet the many people that participate in a trial, and learn about their important jobs.

Kids Discover: The Supreme Court
http://www.kidsdiscover.com/spotlight/supreme-court-kids
=/?c_cid=1cf9ce78ac&mc_eid=369e19759c
Look inside the Supreme Court. Learn about the justices, and discover fun facts about the highest court in the nation.

Index

Photo Acknowledgments

Image credits: Allan Tannenbaum/Getty Images, p. 4; RichLegg/E+/Getty Images, p. 5; Carol M. Highsmith Archive/Library of Congress p. 6; Fred Schilling/Collection of the Supreme Court of the United States, p. 7; Chuck Kennedy/The White House, p. 8; Win McNamee/Getty Images, p. 9; Comstock/Stockbyte/Getty Images, p. 10; monkeybusinessimages/iStock/Getty Images, p. 11; National Archives, p. 12; Congressional Quarterly/Getty Images, p. 13; Monkey Business Images/Shutterstock.com, p. 14; Library of Congress, p. 15; Justin Sullivan/Getty Images, p. 16; Pool/Getty Images, p. 17; Brooks Kraft/Getty Images, p. 20; Joyce N. Boghosian/ The White House, p. 18; Library of Congress LC-USZ62-44543, p. 19; Hero Images/Getty Images, pp. 21, 25; Dawn Shearer-Simonetti/Shutterstock.com, p. 22; Jose Luis Pelaez Inc/ DigitalVision/Getty Images, p. 23; Miami Herald/Getty Images, p. 24; AP Photo/Jon Elswick, p. 26; wavebreakmedia/Shutterstock.com, p. 27; Rob Marmion/Shutterstock.com, p. 28.

Cover: SAUL LOEB/Getty Images.